MINEX II

Performance of Fingerprint Match-on-Card Algorithms
Phase II Report

NIST Interagency Report 7477

P. Grother, W. Salamon, C. Watson, M. Indovina, and P. Flanagan

Information Access Division

National Institute of Standards and Technology

February 29, 2008

Executive Summary

The MINEX II trial was conducted to evaluate the accuracy and speed of MATCH-ON-CARD verification algorithms. These run on ISO/IEC 7816 smartcards. They compare conformant reference and verification instances of the ISO/IEC 19794-2 COMPACT CARD fingerprint minutia standard. The test therefore represents an assessment of the core viability of the de facto leading compact biometric data element on personal identity credentials based on the the industry standard smart card. The results are relevant to users seeking to use minutia templates as an additional factor for authentication.

MINEX II did not evaluate interface standards, secure transmission protocols, nor card or algorithm vulnerabilities. In addition, it did not mimic a particular verification scenario, and it did not compare fingerprint sensors or system-on-card implementations. More generally an exposition of the advantages and disadvantages of MATCH-ON-CARD is beyond the scope of this report. Also out-of-scope is consideration of modalities beyond fingerprints[3].

The significant results of the test are below. The authors are available to talk about this report.

▷ The most accurate MATCH-ON-CARD implementation achieves the minimum error rate specifications of the United States' Government's PIV program. — Sec. 4.4

▷ For the one provider who has submitted both MATCH-ON-CARD and MATCH-OFF-CARD minutiae matching algorithms to NIST, the accuracy of the former approaches that of the latter. — Sec. 4.2

▷ The most accurate MATCH-ON-CARD implementation executes 50% of genuine ISO/IEC 7816 VERIFY commands in 0.54 seconds (i.e. median), and 99% within 0.86 seconds. For the fastest implementation, these values are 0.18 and 0.48 seconds respectively. — Sec. 5

▷ False non-match errors, at the industry preferred false match rate of 0.0001, are from two to four times more frequent than at $FMR = 0.01$. — Sec. 4.4

▷ As in MINEX 04, the use of two fingers greatly improves accuracy. Using OR-rule fusion at a fixed operating threshold, the effect of using a second finger only after a rejection of the first, is to reduce false rejection while increasing false acceptance. — Sec. 4.6

▷ Using OR-rule fusion with the most accurate implementation and targeting $FMR = 0.001$, it is necessary to employ the second finger for fewer than 4% of genuine users. — Sec. 4.7

▷ Some MATCH-ON-CARD implementations emit only a few unique matcher scores. This precludes fine-grained setting of the operating threshold. This disadvantages those implementations because overly conservative FMR values give rise to elevated FNMR. — Sec. 4.8

▷ Some cards indicated a capability to accept no more than 60 points, and this necessitates removal of minutiae from either or both of the reference and verification templates prior to transmission to the card in 16.5 % of genuine comparisons. The use of minutia quality values for removal is superior to using radial distance alone. — Sec. 4.9

▷ MINEX II attained unprecedented transparency in its execution: the evaluation plan was published during its development with industry, and version-controlled open-source software was released for both conformance and conversion of INCITS 378 and ISO/IEC 19794-2 COMPACT CARD templates, and for invocation of ISO/IEC 7816 MATCH-ON-CARD operations. — Sec. 3.5

▷ The MINEX II evaluation will continue in 2008 as Phase III. This will be an ongoing program to gauge improvements over existing implementations, and to evaluate others.
NIST invites comment on whether Phase III should include evaluation of proprietary templates, or extensions to ISO/IEC 7816 templates. MINEX 04 showed that MATCH-OFF-CARD algorithms were substantially more accurate with proprietary vs. standard templates. Whether this holds for MATCH-ON-CARD has not been reported. Comments and inquiries are welcome via MINEXII@NIST.GOV.

▷ A number of caveats apply to the quantitative results and conclusions of this report. — Pg. 2

| MX2D = Sagem Morpho | MX2E = Sagem Morpho | MX2G = Oberthur / id3 | MX2H = Oberthur / id3 |
| MX2I = Oberthur / id3 | MX2J = Oberthur / id3 | MX2K = Oberthur / id3 | MX2M = Giesecke - Devrient |

Caveats

As with all biometric evaluations, the results of this test must be carefully interpreted before any predictive conclusions can be made. Users should factor the following into policy, planning and operational decisions.

1. The absolute error rates quoted herein were measured by using the provided implementations on a fixed corpus of operational fingerprint images. However, error rates observed in real-world applications are strongly dependent on a number of factors legitimately not reflected in the experimental design of MINEX II. Among these are:

    ▷ Environment - For instance, low humidity is associated with higher false rejection;
    ▷ Number of verification attempts - More attempts lead to lower false rejection, and higher false acceptance;
    ▷ Number of images used, and the fusion policy - If several images from a sequence are matched, accuracy can be improved;
    ▷ Number of fingers used, and the fusion policy - If images from two or more fingers are used, accuracy is improved;
    ▷ Demographics - Younger adult populations are widely considered to be easier to match;
    ▷ Habituation - Users who regularly interact with a system experience lower rejection rates;
    ▷ The sensor, and the enrollment policy - The application of quantitative quality criteria, e.g. in an auto-capture loop, improves error rates;
    ▷ The data format in use - Proprietary templates generally offer superior error rates to standardized formats[7], but are non-interoperable. Proprietary extensions to standard templates are similarly non-interoperable unless executable code for each vendor's extensions is built into the reader or read from the card.

2. With respect to MOC specifically, the accuracy and speed of operational verification transactions will generally depend on a number of factors, including the following.

    ▷ The operational card stock in use.
    ▷ The number of templates stored on the card.
    ▷ The number of fingers presented.
    ▷ The quality of the enrollment procedure particularly whether a verification was done at time of card issuance.
    ▷ The communications channel and interface.
    ▷ The cryptographic operations needed to secure the channel and to authenticate the card and data elements (but see SBMOC in 1.4).

In addition, the template generation and matching algorithms are strongly influential on error rates. To the extent that MINEX II measured the accuracy of leading industrial and academic algorithms (i.e. only partially), these aspects are documented here. Thus this MINEX trial addresses the core algorithmic capability of a MOC implementation. The results:

▷ support qualification processes (e.g. PIV),
▷ have relevance operationally (matching accuracy and speed are strongly *influential* components of a system),
▷ are not sufficient for prediction of fielded performance.

Disclaimer

Specific hardware and software products identified in this report were used in order to perform the evaluations described in this document. In no case does identification of any commercial product, trade name, or vendor, imply recommendation or endorsement by the National Institute of Standards and Technology, nor does it imply that the products and equipment identified are necessarily the best available for the purpose.

Release Notes

▷ The MINEX II evaluation was conducted in accordance with the MINEX II Specification which has been released as a separate NIST Interagency Report, NISTIR 7485. The plan was developed by NIST in consultation with members of the fingerprint and smart card industries, and the general public. The document was drafted in April 2007, and finalized on August 15, 2007. The new NISTIR version adds only a note on context, a coversheet, and acknowledgements to it. It is being referred to here because the document is cited herein, and because it is a suitable protocol for other organizations wishing to evaluate MATCH-ON-CARD implementations.

▷ Thoughout this report the names of the vendors are associated with a single letter. This association was instantiated to support automated administration of the test and to effect a containment of the vendor identities within specific personnel at NIST. The letter codes were assigned in approximate order of receipt of the implementation and its passing of subsequent validation and conformance trials. The use of these letters is maintained in this report to conserve space in its many tables. For reference, the letters are associated with the providers' names in a running footnote.

▷ A glossary of terms and definitions is given on page 4.

▷ Much of the tabulated content in this report was produced automatically. This involved the use of scripting tools to generate directly typesettable LaTeX content. This improves timeliness, flexibility and maintainability, and reduces transcription errors.

▷ This PDF file is likely to be better viewed in print than on-screen.

▷ Readers are asked to direct any correspondence regarding this report to the MINEXII@NIST.GOV.

Acknowledgements

The authors would like to thank the Department of Homeland Security's Science and Technology Directorate as sponsors of this work.

The authors would like to take this opportunity to again thank those individuals and organizations identified in the MINEX II evaluation plan [8] for the contributions toward the initiation of this work.

Terms and Definitions

Table 1 gives MINEX-specific definitions to various words and acronyms found in this report.

No.	Term	Definition
1	ANSI	American National Standards Institute
2	ISO	International Organization for Standardization
3	IEC	International Electrotechnical Commission
4	SC 17	Subcommittee responsible for development of indentfication card standards
5	SC 37	Subcommittee responsible for development of biometrics standards
6	INCITS	International Committee for Information Technology Standards
7	INCITS 378:2004	U.S. standard governing the templates
8	ISO/IEC 19795-2:2005	International variant of the INCITS 378 format
9	Compact card	Three-bytes per minutia format defined in ISO/IEC 19794-2:2005
10	Standard template	Record containing standard $(x, y, \theta, type, quality)$ minutiae
11	Proprietary template	Template comparable only with a template from the same vendor
12	Enrollment template	Synonym for reference template
13	Reference template	Template from the first sample of a subject, stored on card
14	Authentication template	Template generated from a second sample of a subject, or from an impostor's sample
15	Matcher	Software function that compares two templates to produce a similarity score
16	Generator	Software function that accepts an image and produces a template
17	Native matching	Comparison by matcher from vendor X of two templates from vendor X's generator
18	BIT	Biometric Information Template (See ISO/IEC 7816)
19	BDB	Biometric Data Block (See SC37's *Harmonized Vocabulary*[1])
20	Genuine	Comparison of templates from the same person
21	Impostor	Comparison of templates from different individuals
22	Verification	One-to-one comparison
23	Authentication	Synonym for verification
24	FAR	False accept rate (i.e. transactional outcome)
25	FRR	False reject rate (i.e. transactional outcome)
26	FMR	False match rate (i.e. 1:1 single sample comparison outcome)
27	FNMR	False non-match rate (i.e. 1:1 single sample comparison outcome)
28	DET	Detection Error Tradeoff characteristic
29	SDK	Software Development Kit
30	APDU	Application Protocol Data Unit
31	API	Application Programming Interface
32	DHS	U. S. Department of Homeland Security
33	NIST	National Institute of Standards and Technology
34	POE	Referring to samples collected in a port of entry
35	BVA	Referring to samples collected as part of a biometric visa application
36	MINEX	The Minutiae Interoperability Exchange program

Table 1: Glossary of MINEX II related terms

1 Introduction

The approval of the U.S. and international fingerprint minutia template standards, specifically INCITS 378 and ISO/IEC 19794-2:2005, have created the possibility to establish an interoperable multivendor marketplace for applications involving fast, economic, and accurate interchange and matching of compact biometric templates.

The standards are not application specific. They define formats which can be used for both MATCH-OFF-CARD and MATCH-ON-CARD. While the viability of the templates for MATCH-OFF-CARD has been assessed previously [7, 6, 5], the MATCH-ON-CARD application, which is almost always conceived of as occuring on conformant ISO/IEC 7816 smart cards, has not been independently and publicly tested.

Thus, the MINEX II trial was designed to answer three important and outstanding questions surrounding MATCH-ON-CARD, namely:

▷ What is the accuracy loss incurred using the three bytes per minutia ISO/IEC 19794-2 COMPACT CARD format favored for MATCH-ON-CARD, vs. the six bytes per minutia INCITS 378 format?

▷ What loess in accuracy is incurred when fingerprint minutia templates are matched on ISO/IEC 7816 cards vs. on a resource-rich processor?

▷ What is the time needed to execute the algorithmic matching operation?

The first question was addressed in the MINEX II Evaluation Plan [8]. While the last question can be estimated by ad hoc usage, it is the near-term imperative to answer the second question that served as the primary motivator for the MINEX II study.

The results of MINEX II may have implications for projects such as the US Government's Personal Identity Verification (PIV) program[1] and the U.S. Department of Homeland Security's Transportation Worker Identification Credential (TWIC). PIV was initiated by Homeland Security Presidential Directive 12[2]. This mandated the establishment of a common identification standard for federal employees and contractors. It required interoperable use of identity credentials to control physical and logical access to federal government facilities and systems. In response, NIST released FIPS 201[3] in February 2005, which includes the definition of an identity credential. It specified the inclusion of data from two fingerprints as a third authentication factor. The format for this information was finalized in February 2006, when NIST *Special Publication 800-76* specified the MINEX II profile of the INCITS 378 standard. A broad timeline is given in Table 2.

1.1 MINEX background

The wider MINEX program is intended to improve template-based interoperability from the imperfect state reported in MINEX 04 and MTIT[6] toward that achievable with image-based implementations. The approach is to conduct several programs, MINEX II, III, IV etc, each of which will embed development, evaluation, targeted feedback and consultation activities between NIST, industry and other interested parties. Within scope are any issues to do with fingerprint minutiae as an interoperable biometric. Typical outcomes will be measurements of accuracy, processing time, template size, and commentary on the relevant standards, studies of utility of quality measures, calibration information, and new metrics. Two prior tests have been conducted:

▷ **MINEX 04** was conducted as an initial comparison of image vs. minutia-based interoperability. It assessed the core algorithmic ability of fingerprint matcher Z to compare minutiae templates from sources X and Y. It compared the matching accuracy in that case with fully proprietary templates on the same sets of archival images. The test adopted the INCITS 378 template as a base standard. The test is now closed. http://fingerprint.nist.gov/minex04

---
[1] See http://csrc.nist.gov/piv-program/
[2] The text of HSPD 12 is here: http://www.whitehouse.gov/news/releases/2004/08/20040827-8.html
[3] See Federal Information Processing Standards Publication 201, *Personal Identity Verification for Federal Employees and Contractors* and related documents here: http://csrc.nist.gov/piv-program

No.	Period	Event
1	August 25 1986	Minutiae standardization begins: ANSI/NBS[5]-ICST 1-1986 Data Format for Fingerprint Information Interchange standard.
2	December 12 2003	Initial discussions for MINEX 04 at NIST
3	March 8 2004	INCITS 378 Finalized
4	August 27 2004	Homeland Security Presidential Directive 12 is signed
5	September 21 2004	MINEX 04 is announced publicly
6	September 15 2005	Publication of ISO/IEC 19794-2 Biometric Data Interchange Format - Finger minutiae data
7	December 2005	Amendments to INCITS 378 discussed in Toronto meeting of M1
8	February 1 2006	NIST Special Publication 800-76-1 is released
9	March 6 2006	MINEX 04 , NISTIR 7296, is released
10	March 6 2006	ONGOING MINEX is announced
11	March 12 2007	MINEX II Concept document released for comment
12	August 15 2007	MINEX II Test Plan finalized
13	October 14 2007	MINEX II Phase I results returned to suppliers
14	November 15 2007	MINEX II Phase II submission deadline
15	January 16 2008	MINEX II Phase II report is submitted for release

Table 2: MINEX chronology and related events.

▷ **Ongoing MINEX** is a continuing program of interoperability assessment intended to measure conformance and interoperability of INCITS 378:2004 samples. The test uses one expanded partition of the MINEX 04 data to formulate interoperable groups of matchers and template generators. One client of Ongoing MINEX is the US Government's PIV program which has its own set of criteria against which the interoperable group is formed. The test results are available to other applications or programs which may elect to set their own criteria for interoperable performance. The test remains open[4]

1.2 MINEX II objectives

The MINEX 04 evaluation was intended to assess the viability of the INCITS 378 templates as the interchange medium for fingerprint data. The main objective was to determine whether standardized minutia reference templates can be subsequently matched against an authentication template from another vendor. MINEX II retains this objective but focuses the activity to a restricted class of matchers.

MINEX II is intended to measure the core algorithmic capabilities of fingerprint matching algorithms running on standardized ISO/IEC 7816 smart cards. Specifically the MINEX II program has

▷ instantiated a mechanism for MATCH-ON-CARD testing,

▷ measured the accuracy of MATCH-ON-CARD implementations using ISO/IEC 19794-2:2005 compact card minutia templates,

▷ timed the various operations, and

▷ demonstrated the viability of INCITS 378:2004 as a parent to the ISO/IEC 19794-2 compact card. This leveraged transcoding code residing in NIST's open-source BIOMDI (Biometric Data Interchange) repository[6].

The following are specifically not within the current scope of this evaluation.

▷ The ISO/IEC 19794-2 "record" and "card normal" templates.

▷ Ridge count, core and delta, and zonal quality extensions.

---

[4]For results and participation see http://fingerprint.nist.gov/minex.
[6]See http://biometrics.nist.gov/nigos

Card Vendor	Fingerprint Matcher Vendor	Vendor IDs		NIST IDs	Phase I		Phase II	
					Generator	Matcher	Generator	Matcher
TecSec	Precise Biometrics	00990100	000B0100	MX2A		+		
TecSec	Precise Biometrics	00990101	000B0101	MX2B		+		
Internet Risk Management	Neurotechnologija	00312001	00312001	MX2C	+			
Sagem Morpho	Sagem Morpho	001D6221	001D0002	MX2D	+	+	+	+
Sagem Morpho	Sagem Morpho	001D6221	001D0003	MX2E	+	+	+	+
Oberthur	ID 3	0415010B	003F0301	MX2F		+		+
Oberthur	ID 3	0415010C	003F0108	MX2G		+		+
Oberthur	ID 3	0415010C	003F0109	MX2H		+		+
Oberthur	ID 3	0415010C	003F0216	MX2I		+		+
Oberthur	ID 3	0415010C	003F0222	MX2J		+		+
Oberthur	ID 3	0415010C	003F0228	MX2K		+		+
Giesecke & Devrient	Giesecke & Devrient	41570001	41570010	MX2M				+

Table 3: Teams entering MINEX II Phases I and II.
Only Phase II results are published. A "+" indicates which components the team elected to provide: The template generator was optional, the matcher was mandatory. Empty cells indicate the provider elected not to participate, or failed to submit according to the deadline.

▷ Proprietary templates, and non-standard extensions to any standardized minutia format.

▷ Evaluation of readers, including performance, conformance and interoperability.

▷ Evaluation of ruggedness or durability of the card.

▷ On-card template generation (i.e. extraction of minutiae from images).

▷ Template update or adaptation.

▷ A formal test of conformance to parts of ISO/IEC 7816. However, the test uses ISO/IEC 7816 parts 4 and 11, and conformance to the relevant clauses thereof was required.

▷ Devices not conforming to ISO/IEC 7816, including all system-on-card and sense-on-card devices embedding proprietary templates[7].

1.3 Participation

With the primary MINEX II objective to ascertain MATCH-ON-CARD capability by measuring fingerprint algorithm accuracy in the intended environment (i.e. the card), the test allowed card vendors to team with several fingerprint algorithm vendors, and vice versa. This policy reflected the notion that if accuracy can be traded against speed, then a fingerprint supplier's technology may demonstrate improved accuracy when implemented on a more capable card. NIST therefore required identification of both the card and fingerprint technology suppliers, and these are presented in Table 3. Note

▷ The teams participating in MINEX II are identified by their full name in Table 3, and by a letter code and an abbreviated name in the running footer of each page.

▷ The test was conducted in two phases. The first was intended as a preliminary small scale test with release of results only to the provider. Per the participation agreement[8], Table 3 indicates the names of the teams in both phases. One team elected to participate only in Phase II. Two others withdrew after Phase I.

▷ Participants were encouraged, but not required, to supply an INCITS 378 fingerprint minutia template generator. One elected to do so.

---

[7]These devices should only be tested in a live scenario test, with device instrumentation to capture proprietary templates for offline cross-comparison.

Fingerprint Vendor	NIST ID	IBIA ID
Cogent	A	00170A47
Dermalog	B	000D088E
Bioscrypt	C	00020004
Sagem Morpho	D	001D0100
Neurotechnologija	E	00310100
Innovatrics	F	00350A01
NEC	G	00118201
Cross Match Technologies	N	00180406
L1/Identix	1C	000C0D60
Precise Biometrics	1D	000B0100
XTec	1F	00340035
SecuGen	1G	000A0035
BIO-key International	1J	00300258
Motorola	1L	002E0101
Aware	1M	003B0101
Sonda Technologies	1N	003C0101
Neurotechnologija	1T	00310101
Aware	1Y	003B0102
ImageWare	2A	00430011

Table 4: Suppliers of Ongoing MINEX compliant template generators

▷ In addition INCITS 378 templates from the suppliers listed in Table 4 were used. Most of these suppliers did not take part in the MINEX II evaluation but their templates are archived in support of the ONGOING MINEX program[8].

1.4 Relationship to NIST's SBMOC activity

A concurrent and related but procedurally separate activity, SECURE BIOMETRIC MATCH-ON-CARD (SBMOC) FEASIBILITY STUDY was conducted at NIST[9] asa a demonstration of MATCH-ON-CARD authentication in which the communications channel was secured, the privacy and integrity of the biometric data was cryptographically protected and the card was authenticated to the reader, and this was done using a contactless interface. The operations were timed, with the goal of conducting an authentication within 2.5 seconds. The results have been published as NISTIR 7452 *Secure Biometric Match-on-Card Feasibility Report* [4].

Not all participants in the SBMOC entered MINEX II , and vice versa.

2 Test implementation

2.1 Concept

The MINEX II evaluation measures MATCH-ON-CARD performance at low false match rates with statistical robustness. This necessitates the execution of very large numbers of genuine and impostor comparisons. These cannot be conducted on physical cards for reasons of total time and card durability. Thus, the fundamental approach to testing is to run a PC-based implementation of the card algorithm, and then to verify that the PC algorithm is the same as that on the card by re-running a subset of the template comparisons on the actual card, and checking that the output similarity scores are identical.

---
[8]See http://fingerprint.nist.gov/minex
[9]MINEX II was run by the Information Access Division. The SBMOC activity was conducted by the Computer Security Division.

2.2 Procedures

The test was implemented by requiring participants to submit the minutiae matching algorithm as an SDK conforming to the MINEX II API specification and a card supporting the MINEX II APDUs. Both of these are documented definitively in the accompanying MINEX II Evaluation Plan [8].

NIST authored and released open-source software (see section 3.6) for conversion of INCITS 378 to ISO/IEC 19794-2 COMPACT CARD templates. This operation respected the ISO/IEC 7816-11:2004 Biometric Information Template (BIT) parameters for minutia count, and sort order. This process is described in detail in the evaluation plan [8].

Execution of the test can be summarized as a six stage process:

1. Validation of SDK functionality - This procedure has been document previously [7];

2. Validation of MOC functionality - The MOC procedure is to execute all necessary APDUs and check for errors (see section 6);

3. Use of (optional) SDK template generators to produce INCITS 378 templates, and retrieval of baseline ONGOING MINEX templates from archival storage;

4. Reading and storage of ISO/IEC 7816-11:2004 BIT card capability records from the submitted cards. The salient BIT properties are recorded in Table 12;

5. Execution of off-card (i.e. SDK) matching. This process embeds on-the-fly conversion of INCITS 378 templates to ISO/IEC 19794-2 COMPACT CARD, respecting the BIT. The number of template comparisons was 2747804 for each matcher tested[10]

6. Repetition of 40000 templates comparisons on the card, and crosscheck of matcher scores against the SDK output.

2.3 Fingerprint datasets

A single corpus of fingerprint images was used for MINEX II testing. This is referred to as the POEBVA data set, and it is identical to that described in the MINEX 04 report [7] except that more samples have been drawn from the same population. The dataset is distinguished from many biometric testing corpora in two valuable ways:

▷ First, the enrollment and authentication images are collected at separate locations in different environments with different sensors. The BVA images are collected as part of a non-immigrant visa application process. The POE images are collected later when the subject crosses the U.S. border at a Port of Entry.

▷ Second, the POE authentication images were collected without human intervention in an autocapture process. This embeds an automated quality-in-the-loop assessment to select the best image, ahead of a timeout. This has the effect of elevating overall quality.

Together these aspects enhance the operational relevance of the MINEX II results.

2.4 Interoperabilty

The MINEX II study addressed the conventional logical or physical access paradigm in which a user's smart card, populated with a reference template provided by vendor A and a matching algorithm from vendor B, is used in an authentication attempt in which a template is generated from an acquired image by the generator from a third vendor, C. This tripartite scenario was examined in MINEX 04 and error rates were generally degraded relative to the case where the verification template generator and matcher were provided by the same supplier, as they may well be in off-card matching. Table 5 summarizes typical bipartite and tripartite relationships in federated interoperable applications.

---

[10]This test is repeated for each combination of template generators.

On Card	Off Card
▷ Reference template generator is selected by manufacturer of issuance system, A. Format is ISO/IEC 19794-2 COMPACT CARD. ▷ Matcher is selected by provider of card stock, B. It compares ISO/IEC 19794-2 COMPACT CARD instances. ▷ Verification generator from reader maufacturer, C. It would extract INCITS 378 data, and convert to ISO/IEC 19794-2 COMPACT CARD. ▷ Often $A \neq B \neq C$	▷ Reference template generator is selected by manufacturer of issuance system, A. Format is INCITS 378 or ISO/IEC 19794-2 COMPACT CARD. ▷ Matcher selected by reader manufacturer, B. It compares either INCITS 378 or ISO/IEC 19794-2 COMPACT CARD records. ▷ Verification template generator selected by reader manufacturer, C. It prepares a INCITS 378 instance, possibly supplemented with proprietary features. ▷ Often $A \neq B, B = C$

Table 5: Typical relationships and roles in interoperable applications.

3 Metrics

3.1 Performance measures

This document quantifies accuracy and interoperability in terms of false non-match and false match error rates, FNMR and FMR. The quantities are computed empirically. If s_{ii} denotes a matcher score obtained by comparing two samples from person i, and $N(t)$ is the number of such scores below threshold, t,

$$N(t) = |\{i : s_{ii} < t\}| \qquad (1)$$

then FNMR is the fraction of genuine comparisons for which the score is less than the operating threshold:

$$\text{FNMR}(t) = \frac{N(t)}{N(\infty)} \qquad (2)$$

where $N(-\infty)$ is the number of genuine comparisons conducted. Likewise, if s_{ij} denotes a matcher score obtained by comparing samples from persons i and j, and $M(t)$ is the number of such scores greater than or equal to a threshold, t,

$$M(t) = |\{i : s_{ij} \geq t\}| \qquad i \neq j \qquad (3)$$

then FMR is the fraction of impostor comparisons resulting in a score greater than or equal to the operating threshold

$$\text{FMR}(t) = \frac{M(t)}{M(-\infty)} \qquad (4)$$

where $M(\infty)$ is number of impostor comparisons conducted.

FMR is regarded as a measure of security, i.e. the fraction of illegitmate matching attempts that result in success.

These error rates must be understood as being *matching* error rates, not *transactional* rates. The ISO/IEC SC 37 Working Group 5 has established different terms for these rates: FMR and FNMR refer to comparisons of single samples, while FAR and FRR apply to the outcome of a human-system transaction in which a user might, for example, make multiple attempts and multiple finger placements.

3.2 Thresholds in the DET computation

As is typical in offline testing [2], this report does not fix an operating threshold but instead uses all the scores from a matcher as thresholds that could be used in actual operation.

	Number of unique score values		
	Genuine	Impostor	All
MX2D	18907	7428	19993
MX2E	19544	7503	19996
MX2G	101	24	101
MX2H	110	22	110
MX2I	103	21	103
MX2J	103	21	103
MX2K	103	21	103
MX2M	50	14	50

Table 6: Number of unique similarity scores.

This testing practice contrasts with fielded MATCH-ON-CARD applications in which the card is configured with a fixed operating threshold, against which a *decision* is rendered.

For MINEX II we required the SDK and the card to produce integer matcher scores on at most $[0, 65535]$. The advantage over just producing true-false decisions is that it allows a survey over *all* operating points, t, and the production of a DET characteristic. This is a plot of FNMR(t) against FMR(t)[11] and, as the primary output of a biometric performance test, is vital in establishing the tradeoff between the inconvenience incorrect rejection of legitimate users, and the incorrect acceptance of fraudulent users.

3.3 Thresholds for computation of interoperability matrices

Setting an operational threshold is often a sensitive issue because of implications for security, convenience, throughput, and cost. It is always application specific. Although this report makes no recommendations on threshold setting, it has necessarily adopted "default" performance figures of merit in support of comparison objectives. Unless stated otherwise, the results in this report correspond to the threshold that produces a FMR of 0.01. The figure of merit is the FNMR at that point. The value 0.01 should not be construed as a recommended operating point but as a value at which error rate differences may be readily observed.

The interoperability matrices show FNMR for fixed FMR values, e.g. $f = 0.01$. However, this requires the computation of FNMR(t_0) for $t_0 = $ FMR$^{-1}(f)$, and while this is trivial for continuous matcher scores it is not so for tied integer scores. The inverse FMR computation is approximate because there is no value for which FMR(t_0) is exactly f. So the threshold actually used, t, is the lowest observed score value for which FMR$(t) \leq f$. In some cases this yields FMR values substantially below the target f. This is a conservative policy decision in the sense that FMR is on the "safe" side of f.

This issue is especially apparent in MATCH-ON-CARD implementations because, as Table 6 shows, some algorithms emit only a limited number of unique scores, perhaps as a result of some need to to conserve computational resources. The values are observations over $O(10^7)$ comparisons. In principle, each value can be used as a threshold against which acceptance and rejection decisions are based. The lack of possible impostor values precludes a fine grained setting of security policy. The MINEX 04 matchers exhibited many more unique values. The fused scores used in Table 8 take on more unique values because of the eq.(6) sum.

This issue is not critical for DETs, which plot the error rates at all possible thresholds with straight lines connecting them. Note, that theory indicates [12] that points on the convex hull of the DET curve between two operating thresholds are accessible by randomly using one or the other for each comparison. The operational use of this practice is not known.

3.4 Handling failure to enroll

The MINEX test protocols have all required template generators to produce a standard template whatever the input image. Thus if a template generator was presented with an image of such poor quality that it would operationally reject

---

[11] DET characteristics sometimes plot Normal deviates, i.e. a plot in which the FNMR and FMR are (nonlinearly) transformed by the inverse CDF of $N(0,1)$. This is abandoned here because the score densities are not Normal.

| MX2D = Sagem Morpho | MX2E = Sagem Morpho | MX2G = Oberthur / id3 | MX2H = Oberthur / id3 |
| MX2I = Oberthur / id3 | MX2J = Oberthur / id3 | MX2K = Oberthur / id3 | MX2M = Giesecke - Devrient |

it (i.e. a failure to enroll), the output in MINEX II is nevertheless required to be a template that is a valid input to the matcher. The template is allowed to contain zero minutiae. Such templates are formally conformant to INCITS 378.

When a SDK-based or MOC-based algorithm is presented with a zero minutiae template it will produce a low similarity score (e.g. zero). The effect of this in an impostor comparison is a correct rejection and improved FMR. For a genuine transaction, the result is a false non-match and degraded FNMR.

3.5 Open-source support for MOC

MINEX II demonstrated an unprecedented level of openness in its evaluation methods. Specifically the test plan was developed in conjunction with industry and both the template conversion and MATCH-ON-CARD test harness were fully open during their development phase, as decribed below.

3.6 Support for biometric data interchange standards

The BIOMDI open source project[12] contains several software library and program packages for handling records specified in INCITS and ISO biometric data format standards. The MINEX II test program uses the finger minutia package to process the INCITS 378 records, converting them to ISO compact card format. In addition, several tools in this package are used to validate the records, or simply to view them.

3.7 Support for MATCH-ON-CARD implementations

The BIOMAPP open source project[13] contains the source code for the match on card test drivers, the tag-length-value (TLV) object processing, and an example SDK test driver. The programs within the BIOMAPP project make use of the finger minutiae libraries from the BIOMDI project. Also, the card test driver utilizes the pcsclite library described in Appendix A.

The goal of the BIOMAPP match on card package is to achieve independence from any particular vendor's middleware. The software communicates directly with the card at the APDU level, removing any need for a middleware API or custom smart card software.

4 MOC Accuracy

4.1 Uncertainty estimates

This section includes estimates of various false non-match rate (FNMR) and false match rates (FMR). These were estimated over fixed numbers of template comparisons.

- ▷ For single finger matching, the number of genuine and impostor comparisons was 247924 and 2499880 respectively corresponding to the use of two impressions of each of the left and right index fingers of 123962 unique subjects. The left index finger from each subject was compared with upto ten other left index fingers. The right index finger was compared with the right index finger of the same individuals. Each finger of each subject was used in only one genuine comparison.

- ▷ For two-finger matching, the number of genuine and impostor comparisons was 123962 and 1249940. Again subjects were reused upto ten times.

---

[12]See http://biometrics.nist.gov/nigos
[13]Ibid.

| MX2D = Sagem Morpho | MX2E = Sagem Morpho | MX2G = Oberthur / id3 | MX2H = Oberthur / id3 |
| MX2I = Oberthur / id3 | MX2J = Oberthur / id3 | MX2K = Oberthur / id3 | MX2M = Giesecke - Devrient |

	FMR = 0.01		FMR = 0.001		FMR = 0.0001	
	D	MX2D	D	MX2D	D	MX2D
A	0.0022	0.0038	0.0040	0.0068	0.0068	0.0116
B	0.0017	0.0020	0.0029	0.0036	0.0048	0.0061
D	0.0012	0.0015	0.0022	0.0026	0.0037	0.0041
E	0.0030	0.0040	0.0054	0.0069	0.0084	0.0111
F	0.0025	0.0030	0.0042	0.0054	0.0060	0.0090
G	0.0023	0.0025	0.0040	0.0046	0.0063	0.0080
N	0.0045	0.0049	0.0075	0.0084	0.0123	0.0142
1C	0.0022	0.0030	0.0037	0.0055	0.0065	0.0086
1D	0.0040	0.0052	0.0067	0.0094	0.0104	0.0154
1F	0.0042	0.0046	0.0069	0.0087	0.0121	0.0140
1J	0.0025	0.0032	0.0040	0.0056	0.0056	0.0087
1L	0.0017	0.0023	0.0030	0.0044	0.0054	0.0075
1M	0.0020	0.0022	0.0033	0.0039	0.0056	0.0067
1N	0.0027	0.0038	0.0048	0.0067	0.0072	0.0114
1T	0.0018	0.0022	0.0031	0.0042	0.0047	0.0068
1Y	0.0019	0.0020	0.0032	0.0039	0.0050	0.0062
Ratio	1.23		1.31		1.35	

Table 7: Comparison of MATCH-OFF-CARD (c. 2004) and MATCH-ON-CARD (c. 2007) matchers, "D" and "MX2D". The values are two-finger sum-fused FNMR values for three FMR operating points. Cells are colored red when the PIV FNMR ≤ 0.01 criterion is not met. The matchers are Sagem Morpho's D and MX2D algorithms. The template generators are identified in the rows.

The error rates follow binomial statistics, such that if experiments of the same size were repeated using samples drawn from the same population then, with 95% coverage, the error rate measurement would fall between $p - u \leq p \leq p + u$ where p is the true error rate,

$$u = \Phi^{-1}(1 - \alpha/2)\sqrt{p(1-p)/N} \qquad (5)$$

and $\alpha = 0.05$. This Normal approximation to the binomial distribution leads to the following estimates of uncertainty.

▷ for FMR = $p = 0.0001, N = 1249940, u = 0.00002$,

▷ for FMR = $p = 0.01, N = 1249940, u = 0.0002$, and

▷ for FNMR = $p = 0.01, N = 123962, u = 0.0006$.

▷ for FNMR = $p = 0.1, N = 123962, u = 0.0017$.

These estimates apply to the population of fingerprints identified in 2.3 and do not represent systematic effects associated with the caveats identified on page 2.

4.2 Match-on-Card vs. Match-off-Card

Only one vendor has elected to submit matching algorithms to NIST's on-card MINEX II *and* off-card MINEX 04 trials. Table 7 shows accuracy for the two implementations: While many of the differences are small and not, in isolation, statistically significant the MATCH-OFF-CARD error rates are *all* lower than the MATCH-ON-CARD rates. The last row of the Table shows the ratio of the total false non-matches if all the generators were used in equal proportion. The result is that the MATCH-ON-CARD algorithm produces about 20% to 40% more false non-matches than the provider's MATCH-OFF-CARD implementation [14]. This effect appears to be larger at lower FMR values. This intra-vendor difference in accuracy is substantially less than the inter-vendor differences reported in Table 8. These observations apply to standard templates only.

NIST has not measured accuracy of the MATCH-OFF-CARD implementation since the MINEX 04 implementation was submitted in 2004.

---

[14] Note that ratio measurements have larger undertainties associated with them.

Note that Sagem-Morpho had submitted the matcher with NIST designation 1E to ONGOING MINEX in 2006 under the name "Morpho Match-on-Card, Software Version 1.0". It attained the PIV accuracy specification[15]. Its FNMR performance differs from the MX2D implementation tested here by only ±0.0003. Differences may be attributed to

▷ the use ISO/IEC 19794-2 COMPACT CARD templates here vs. INCITS 378 templates in ONGOING MINEX, and

▷ the larger number of impostor comparisons here (1249940) vs. ONGOING MINEX (124994).

Thus, we conclude that the 2006 implementation submitted for PIV evaluation was indeed the MATCH-ON-CARD algorithm submitted here.

4.3 Comparison of MOC implementations

Figure 1 shows the Detection Error Tradeoff characteristics for the MATCH-ON-CARD implementations tested. The top and bottom plots show, respectively, the result for single finger, and sum-fused two-finger, verification. We make the following observations.

▷ There is a large variation in accuracy between MATCH-ON-CARD matchers. In the operationally interesting range $0.0001 \leq $ FMR $ \leq 0.01$ the rows of Table 8 show that the most accurate implementations demonstrate FNMR values a factor of ten or more smaller than the least accurate.

▷ In the operationally interesting range $0.0001 \leq $ FMR $ \leq 0.01$ the curves do not cross. Thus, if one matcher is more accurate at one threshold, it will also be more accurate elsewhere. This means that *comparative* evaluation of MATCH-ON-CARD implementations at one threshold is substanially representative of another. This result is not generally true however.

▷ False non-match rates FMR $= 0.0001$ are between two and four times worse than those at FMR $= 0.01$.

▷ The two-finger false non-match rates are almost an order of magnitude lower than the single-finger rates.

▷ Accuracy is generally improved when both templates are produced by generator B. The exceptions are for MX2D and MX2E which exhibit better performance when used with the MX2D generator. These two effects are evident in the data reported in the MINEX 04 trial: Matchers give greater accuracy on templates from the same source and to a lesser extent when one of the templates is produced by the matcher provider's template generator.

4.4 Would accuracy be sufficient for PIV compliance?

The question of whether a MATCH-ON-CARD matcher would qualify for the U.S. Government's Personal Identity Verification program is addressed here by subjecting the MATCH-ON-CARD implementation to the NIST Special Publication 800-76-1 interoperable accuracy specification. This states that a matcher submitted for PIV shall be capable of verifying INCITS 378 templates from all previously qualified template generators. This measurement activity is conducted by NIST under the ONGOING MINEX name. The process requires the supplier of the matcher to also submit a template generator. This requirement derives from the MATCH-OFF-CARD situation in which the reader is equipped with a sensor, template generator and matcher. However, because NIST acceded to requests from the industry to allow submission of a MATCH-ON-CARD algorithm without an accompanying template generator, we are only able to conduct the following *simulation* of the PIV assessment process.

We use the current list of ONGOING MINEX qualified template generators to prepare reference templates (notionally for storage on a card), which we then verify against templates from the one MINEX II submitted generator, MX2D, using the MATCH-ON-CARD algorithm under test. This mimics the case in which the supplier of the card were to license and submit Sagem Morpho's template generator to a formal ONGOING MINEX compliance test. The MX2D generator is used

---

[15]The results are posted at http://fingerprint.nist.gov/minex/Results.html

(a) Single finger

(b) Two fingers (sum-rule fusion)

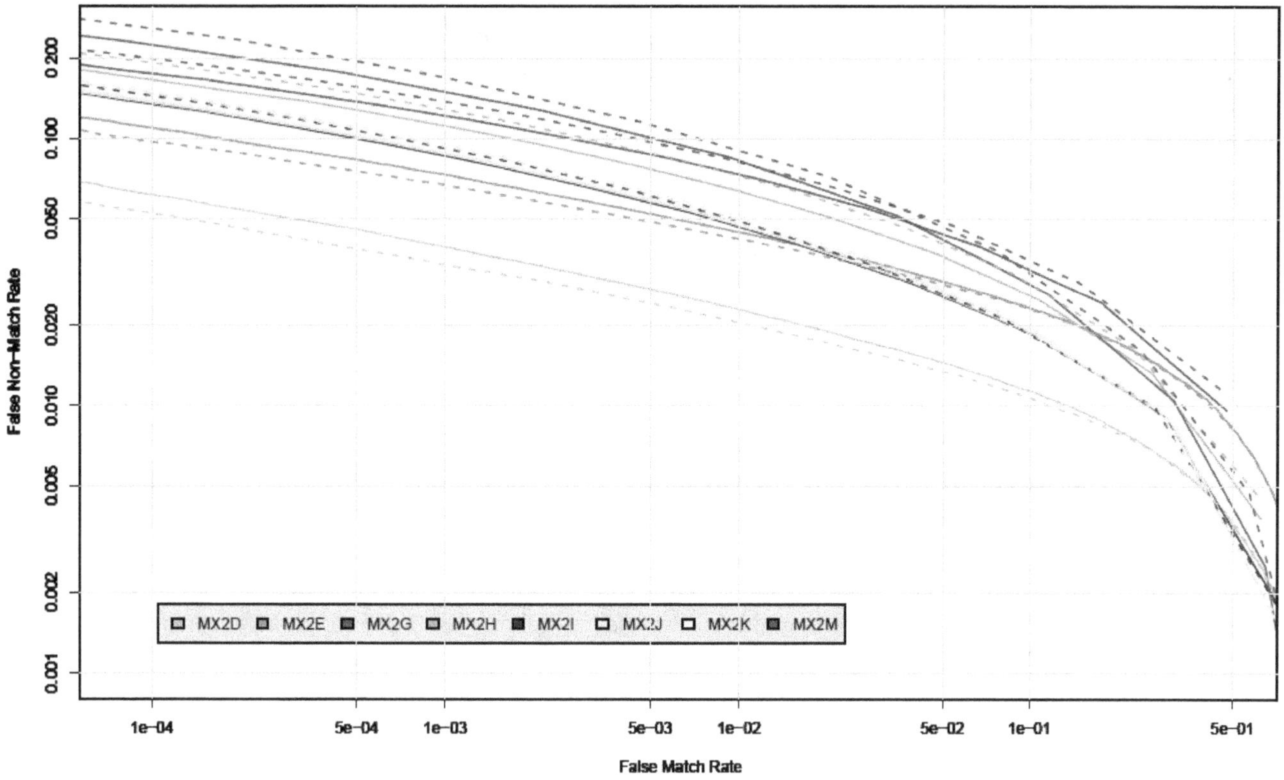

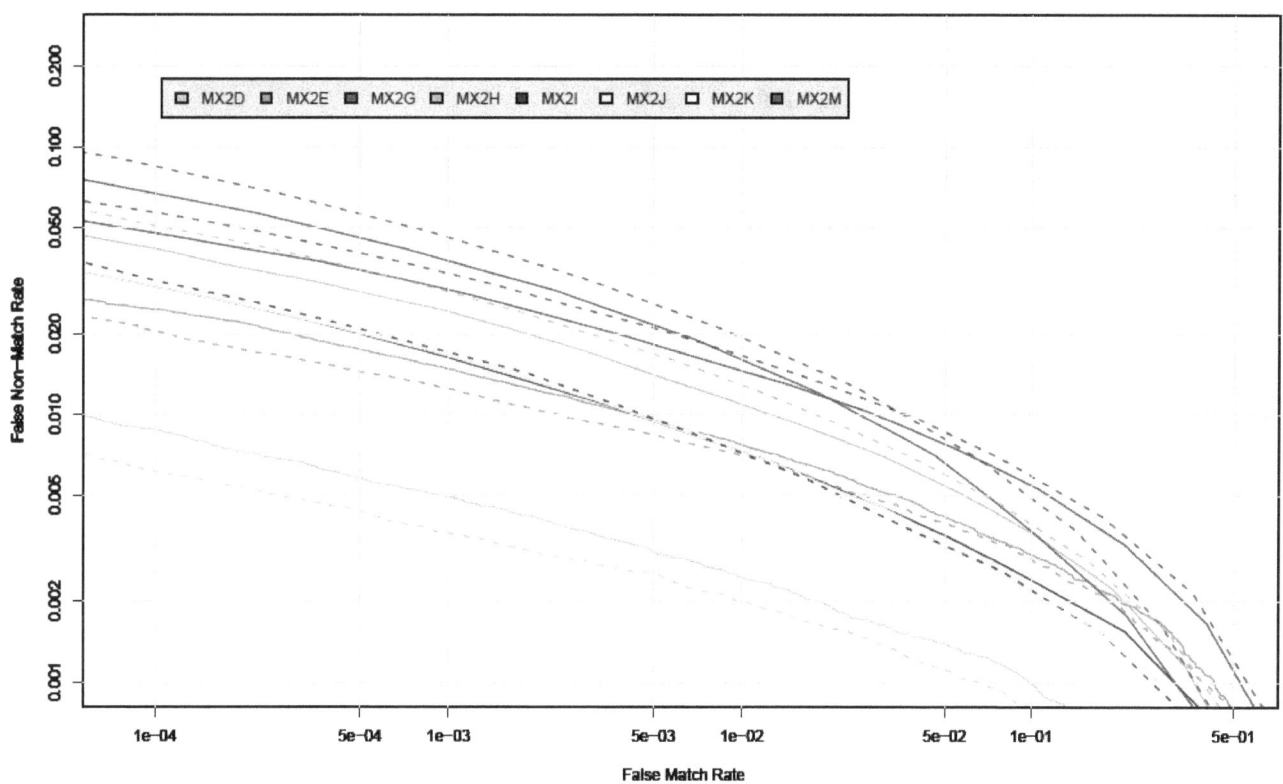

Figure 1: DET characteristics.

The FNMR vs. FMR tradeoffs are shown for two pairs of reference and authentication generators: (B, MX2D) as dashed lines, and (B,B) as solid lines.

MX2D = Sagem Morpho	MX2E = Sagem Morpho	MX2G = Oberthur / id3	MX2H = Oberthur / id3
MX2I = Oberthur / id3	MX2J = Oberthur / id3	MX2K = Oberthur / id3	MX2M = Giesecke - Devrient

because it emits minutia quality values (for BIT use, see section 4.9), is ONGOING MINEX compliant, and because it is was shown in MINEX 04 to yield consistently low error rates in general interoperability situations[16].

We make the following observations.

- From Table 8(a), the complete column of colored cells indicates MX2D would attain compliance with the PIV specification. This confirms the manufacturer's assertion in August 2006 that their succesful[17] ONGOING MINEX submission, 1E, was indeed a MATCH-ON-CARD algorithm.

- Tables 8(b) and 8(d) shows that the implementation would achieve the same FNMR ≤ 0.01 criterion at FMR = 0.001 but not at FMR = 0.0001.

- Three other implmentations, MX2I, MX2J and MX2K come close to attaining PIV compliance. The false non-match rates for some generators exceed the required 0.01 limit.

- The most accurate implementation, MX2D, is more accurate at FMR = 0.0001 than the next best matcher at FMR = 0.01 for all but two template generator combinations (Table 8).

- FNMR values are between two and four times higher at FMR = 0.0001 than at 0.01.

- As documented previously [7, 6, 8] interoperable error rates are higher when three companies are involved (one for the reference template, another for the verification template, and a third for the matcher provider). This is evident in, for example, Table 8 where the native single-vendor element (MX2D, MX2D) error rate is 0.0015 is the most accurate. This arises because of systematic inconsistencies between implementations on which minutiae are true, false, and missed, and on local placement of minutiae.

4.5 The meaning of PIV compliance

For the many reasons noted on page 2, the error rates measured in large scale offline tests using archival data are not specifically representative of any particular application[18].

However single-image matching evaluations, conducted on massive archival data sets, are extremely valuable for:

- fair and repeatable tests,
- comparative assessments of accuracy,
- assessing compliance to a dataset-specific performance threshold, and
- for testing conformance to the standard.

In particular, the offline nature of the ONGOING MINEX and MINEX II tests makes them suitable for assessing the core accuracy and interoperability of minutia matching algorithms. That is, the tests are suitable for exposing implementations that are improperly implementing the underyling INCITS 378 minutia standard.

Thus, while the MINEX trials are necessary for qualification of implementations, and they effectively support operations, they are not sufficient for prediction of fielded performance.

---

[16] In the the Scenario 2 results of the MINEX 04 supplemental http://fingerprint.nist.gov/minex04/minex_scenario2.pdf, many matchers exhibited low error rates when templates from the D generator were matched against arbitrary others.

[17] See http://fingerprint.nist.gov/minex/QPL.html

[18] Except possibly the US-VISIT application, because MINEX II used its images.

| MX2D = Sagem Morpho | MX2E = Sagem Morpho | MX2G = Oberthur / id3 | MX2H = Oberthur / id3 |
| MX2I = Oberthur / id3 | MX2J = Oberthur / id3 | MX2K = Oberthur / id3 | MX2M = Giesecke - Devrient |

Table 8: Compliance to the PIV interoperability specification.

Sum-fused two-finger FNMR values for the interoperable case in which the MINEX II matcher identified in the column compares left and right index finger BVA templates produced by the generator identified in the row, against corresponding POE templates from the MX2D generator. Shaded cells indicate compliance with the PIV error rate specification, FNMR ≤ 0.01 at FMR ≤ 0.01.

(a) FNMR at FMR = 0.01

Nfing	Column = MATCH-ON-CARD algorithm, Row = INCITS 378 generator									
2	MX2D	MX2E	MX2G	MX2H	MX2I	MX2J	MX2K	MX2M
A	0.0038	0.0055	0.0427	0.0324	0.0140	0.0146	0.0156	0.0399
B	0.0020	0.0070	0.0168	0.0159	0.0080	0.0082	0.0086	0.0207
C	0.0030	0.0112	0.0237	0.0231	0.0118	0.0119	0.0128	0.0270
D	0.0015	0.0029	0.0105	0.0066	0.0046	0.0046	0.0048	0.0156
E	0.0040	0.0055	0.0195	0.0143	0.0093	0.0096	0.0102	0.0514
F	0.0030	0.0112	0.0234	0.0225	0.0115	0.0117	0.0125	0.0271
G	0.0025	0.0080	0.0205	0.0152	0.0102	0.0105	0.0083	0.0310
N	0.0049	0.0121	0.0224	0.0168	0.0116	0.0118	0.0123	0.0343
1C	0.0030	0.0054	0.0254	0.0194	0.0087	0.0088	0.0092	0.0425
1D	0.0052	0.0201	0.0315	0.0267	0.0177	0.0181	0.0190	0.0354
1F	0.0046	0.0140	0.0315	0.0248	0.0158	0.0162	0.0170	0.0392
1G	0.0046	0.0140	0.0315	0.0249	0.0158	0.0162	0.0170	0.0393
1J	0.0032	0.0132	0.0272	0.0210	0.0133	0.0133	0.0140	0.0270
1L	0.0023	0.0058	0.0201	0.0146	0.0093	0.0096	0.0101	0.0295
1M	0.0022	0.0056	0.0197	0.0151	0.0071	0.0071	0.0074	0.0268
1N	0.0038	0.0123	0.0290	0.0228	0.0134	0.0136	0.0143	0.0312
1T	0.0022	0.0039	0.0174	0.0130	0.0078	0.0079	0.0060	0.0306
1Y	0.0020	0.0046	0.0166	0.0124	0.0079	0.0080	0.0061	0.0274
2A	0.0030	0.0112	0.0237	0.0231	0.0118	0.0119	0.0128	0.0270

(b) FNMR at FMR = 0.001

Nfing	Column = MATCH-ON-CARD algorithm, Row = INCITS 378 generator								
2	MX2D	MX2E	MX2G	MX2H	MX2I	MX2J	MX2K	MX2M
A	0.0068	0.0105	0.0765	0.0726	0.0325	0.0343	0.0365	0.0808
B	0.0036	0.0125	0.0373	0.0291	0.0178	0.0181	0.0192	0.0479
C	0.0053	0.0190	0.0518	0.0420	0.0247	0.0255	0.0270	0.0589
D	0.0026	0.0053	0.0222	0.0154	0.0099	0.0098	0.0102	0.0342
E	0.0069	0.0099	0.0395	0.0310	0.0186	0.0193	0.0203	0.0956
F	0.0054	0.0189	0.0507	0.0404	0.0241	0.0249	0.0263	0.0586
G	0.0046	0.0135	0.0364	0.0328	0.0207	0.0215	0.0227	0.0673
N	0.0084	0.0197	0.0389	0.0352	0.0228	0.0234	0.0243	0.0717
1C	0.0055	0.0092	0.0446	0.0423	0.0239	0.0250	0.0265	0.0822
1D	0.0094	0.0323	0.0624	0.0536	0.0339	0.0351	0.0367	0.0710
1F	0.0087	0.0237	0.0531	0.0498	0.0306	0.0315	0.0332	0.0798
1G	0.0087	0.0238	0.0531	0.0498	0.0307	0.0316	0.0332	0.0799
1J	0.0056	0.0216	0.0476	0.0378	0.0265	0.0273	0.0230	0.0565
1L	0.0044	0.0106	0.0357	0.0325	0.0192	0.0199	0.0209	0.0608
1M	0.0039	0.0099	0.0341	0.0311	0.0192	0.0196	0.0167	0.0566
1N	0.0067	0.0208	0.0529	0.0510	0.0279	0.0289	0.0302	0.0631
1T	0.0042	0.0071	0.0310	0.0281	0.0164	0.0169	0.0177	0.0617
1Y	0.0039	0.0085	0.0300	0.0272	0.0165	0.0169	0.0177	0.0573
2A	0.0053	0.0190	0.0518	0.0420	0.0247	0.0255	0.0270	0.0589

(c) ONGOING MINEX Compliant Generators

Fingerprint Vendor	NIST ID	IBIA ID
Cogent	A	00170A47
Dermalog	B	000D088E
Bioscrypt	C	00020004
Sagem Morpho	D	001D0100
Neurotechnologija	E	00310100
Innovatrics	F	00350A01
NEC	G	00118201
Cross Match Technologies	N	00180406
L1/Identix	1C	000C0D60
Precise Biometrics	1D	000B0100
XTec	1F	00340035
SecuGen	1G	000A0035
BIO-key International	1J	00300258
Motorola	1L	002E0101
Aware	1M	003B0101
Sonda Technologies	1N	003C0101
Neurotechnologija	1T	00310101
Aware	1Y	003B0102
ImageWare	2A	00430011

(d) FNMR at FMR = 0.0001

Nfing	Column = MATCH-ON-CARD algorithm, Row = INCITS 378 generator								
2	MX2D	MX2E	MX2G	MX2H	MX2I	MX2J	MX2K	MX2M
A	0.0116	0.0177	0.1310	0.1225	0.0701	0.0738	0.0777	0.1394
B	0.0061	0.0205	0.0632	0.0512	0.0366	0.0323	0.0339	0.0901
C	0.0088	0.0300	0.0850	0.0709	0.0435	0.0447	0.0468	0.1061
D	0.0041	0.0085	0.0340	0.0281	0.0176	0.0178	0.0186	0.0647
E	0.0111	0.0158	0.0652	0.0595	0.0371	0.0384	0.0399	0.1240
F	0.0090	0.0305	0.0837	0.0697	0.0493	0.0508	0.0456	0.1058
G	0.0080	0.0209	0.0622	0.0559	0.0400	0.0414	0.0372	0.1222
N	0.0142	0.0297	0.0720	0.0583	0.0433	0.0446	0.0402	0.1239
1C	0.0086	0.0147	0.0784	0.0720	0.0409	0.0425	0.0445	0.1373
1D	0.0154	0.0460	0.0894	0.0857	0.0553	0.0571	0.0596	0.1214
1F	0.0140	0.0358	0.0878	0.0812	0.0502	0.0519	0.0543	0.1362
1G	0.0140	0.0359	0.0879	0.0813	0.0503	0.0520	0.0544	0.1363
1J	0.0087	0.0331	0.0718	0.0649	0.0442	0.0458	0.0477	0.1001
1L	0.0075	0.0178	0.0625	0.0564	0.0333	0.0346	0.0360	0.1086
1M	0.0067	0.0160	0.0583	0.0530	0.0318	0.0326	0.0341	0.1003
1N	0.0114	0.0312	0.0919	0.0862	0.0482	0.0498	0.0519	0.1108
1T	0.0068	0.0120	0.0612	0.0485	0.0281	0.0289	0.0302	0.1065
1Y	0.0062	0.0133	0.0577	0.0470	0.0278	0.0285	0.0300	0.1016
2A	0.0088	0.0300	0.0850	0.0709	0.0435	0.0447	0.0468	0.1061

MX2D = Sagem Morpho	MX2E = Sagem Morpho	MX2G = Oberthur / id3	MX2H = Oberthur / id3
MX2I = Oberthur / id3	MX2J = Oberthur / id3	MX2K = Oberthur / id3	MX2M = Giesecke - Devrient

Matcher	Thresholds t_1	Thresholds t_2	Finger 1 accuracy FMR_1	Finger 1 accuracy FNMR_1	Overall accuracy FMR_T	Overall accuracy FNMR_T	Transaction time, τ_T (s)
MX2D	6298	6298	0.0005	0.0306	0.0010	0.0045	4.59
	6118	6539	0.0007	0.0289	0.0010	0.0044	4.57
MX2E	6338	6338	0.0005	0.0594	0.0010	0.0146	5.67
	6148	6668	0.0007	0.0560	0.0010	0.0146	5.65
MX2G	9	9	0.0004	0.1501	0.0007	0.0466	9.09
	8	10	0.0008	0.1311	0.0009	0.0454	8.87
MX2H	10	10	0.0004	0.1383	0.0008	0.0416	8.57
	9	11	0.0007	0.1211	0.0009	0.0401	8.34
MX2I	9	9	0.0003	0.1025	0.0007	0.0272	7.06
	8	10	0.0007	0.0851	0.0008	0.0261	6.86
MX2J	9	9	0.0003	0.1043	0.0006	0.0280	7.15
	8	9	0.0006	0.0866	0.0010	0.0241	6.69
MX2K	9	9	0.0003	0.1075	0.0006	0.0293	7.28
	8	9	0.0006	0.0893	0.0009	0.0251	6.80
MX2M	11	11	0.0001	0.2202	0.0004	0.0829	12.78
	10	11	0.0007	0.1594	0.0010	0.0629	10.61

Table 9: Simulated expected transaction time for OR-fused two-finger verification.
For each matcher, there are two rows. The first gives the decision level fusion result for equal thresholds ($t_1 = t_2$) with t_1 set to the lowest value for which $\text{FMR}(t_1) \leq 0.0005$. The second row is the result of a minimum cost search over all possible (t_1, t_2) combinations. The last column gives the expected *transaction* time in seconds for the time model given in equation 9. The reference and verification templates are from MX2D and B respectively.

4.6 One and two finger matching

This report contains performance estimates for one and two-finger authentication. The single-finger results are obtained by pooling the scores from the left and right index finger comparisons as though they were from different individuals. The performance estimates are therefore representative of single-finger verification applications in which users choose to present either left or right index fingers in equal proportion. This report does not assess the effect of multiple verification attempts because it uses archived datasets with only two impressions per finger. Note, however, that the images were collected using the auto-capture paradigm in which a number of images were collected over an interval of a few seconds, and the best one (according to a quality assessment algorithm) retained.

Two mechanisms were used for combining two-finger matching scores: score-level fusion, and decision-level fusion.

▷ **Score Fusion:** The fused score is simply the sum of the left and right comparison scores:

$$s_{ij} = s_{ij}^{(R)} + s_{ij}^{(L)} \tag{6}$$

where i and j denote the i-th enrolled image and the j-th authentication sample and s is the scalar output of a matcher. This *sum-rule* is a simple yet powerful method for multi-sample fusion, is ubiquitous in the literature [13, 9], and has long had theoretical recommendation [10]. The fused score is compared against a threshold, and error rates are again computed using eqs. 4 and 2.

The use of fusion, however, has significant implications. In sum-rule fusion, FNMR rates drop substantially for a given FMR but there is the attendant requirement to *always* acquire and match samples from both fingers. This will generally double the time, the exception being if two sensors are available and used simultaneously, whence the total time τ_T

$$\tau_T = \max(\tau_1, \tau_2) \tag{7}$$

where we expect the primary and secondary[19] finger times would be expected to be about the same, i.e. $\tau_1 \approx \tau_2$.

---

[19]We avoid the handedness issue here. In all the analyses we assume each user is righthanded and presents that finger first. This is not true - the natural incidence of right-handedness has been reported as 88%[11] but there are wide geographic and social variations, and a tendency toward righthandness over an individuals lifetime - and is relevant only because left-finger verification gives somewhat larger error rates than right.

	(a) Raw similarity scores						(b) Perturbed similarity scores					
	Single finger		OR fusion		SUM fusion			Single finger		OR fusion		SUM fusion	
Matcher	FMR	FNMR	FMR	FNMR	FMR	FNMR	Matcher	FMR	FNMR	FMR	FNMR	FMR	FNMR
MX2D	0.0005	0.0386	0.0010	0.0045	0.0010	0.0036	MX2D	0.0005	0.0386	0.0010	0.0045	0.0010	0.0036
MX2E	0.0005	0.0753	0.0010	0.0146	0.0010	0.0125	MX2E	0.0005	0.0753	0.0010	0.0146	0.0010	0.0125
MX2G	0.0002	0.1836	0.0007	0.0466	0.0007	0.0373	MX2G	0.0005	0.1579	0.0010	0.0435	0.0010	0.0345
MX2H	0.0002	0.1730	0.0008	0.0416	0.0010	0.0291	MX2H	0.0005	0.1491	0.0010	0.0392	0.0010	0.0287
MX2I	0.0002	0.1353	0.0007	0.0272	0.0009	0.0178	MX2I	0.0005	0.1095	0.0010	0.0245	0.0010	0.0175
MX2J	0.0001	0.1386	0.0006	0.0280	0.0008	0.0181	MX2J	0.0005	0.1108	0.0010	0.0248	0.0010	0.0175
MX2K	0.0001	0.1425	0.0006	0.0293	0.0008	0.0192	MX2K	0.0005	0.1126	0.0010	0.0251	0.0010	0.0180
MX2M	0.0000	0.3016	0.0004	0.0829	0.0009	0.0479	MX2M	0.0005	0.2085	0.0010	0.0675	0.0010	0.0469

Table 10: Use of the second finger.
Accuracy of single-finger, OR-fused ($t_1 = t_2$) and SUM-fused two-finger verification. The threshold is fixed to target a single-finger false match of 0.0005. This is not always achieved (FMR in second column of Table 10(a)) due to discretized similarity scores. The problem disappears in Table 10(b) via addition of noise as described in sec. 4.8. This produces the targeted FMR and reduces FNMR. Cells are shaded when matching of the the reference (MX2D) and verification (B) templates achieves the PIV accuracy specification.

These times would include the user-sensor interaction, capture, minutiae extraction, template generation, communication with smartcard, matching, and return of the result.

If, as is more common, the acquisition is sequential, then the total time, τ_T for sum-rule fusion will be

$$\tau_T = \tau_1 + \tau_2 \tag{8}$$

This approach turns out to be accurate but time consuming for users.

▷ **Decision ("OR") Fusion:** The more efficient alternative is to only conditionally acquire and compare the second finger. That is, if recognition of a genuine user or impostor is unsuccessful with the first finger, then the second finger is acquired and matched. This constitutes decision-level "OR" fusion. The idea is that many genuine users will require only a single finger to authenticate while the FMR security objective is met after one or two fingers are used. We analyse the time-savings by adopting the model of the 2006 NIST study[14] in which the total transaction time per genuine user will be

$$\tau_T = \tau_1 + \tau_2 \text{FNMR}_1(t_1) + \tau_r \text{FNMR}_T(t_1, t_2) \tag{9}$$

where

- t_1 and t_2 are the first and second finger matcher thresholds,
- τ_r is the time taken for the resolution of cases where both fingers fail to match[20],
- $\text{FNMR}_1(t_1)$ is the fraction of genuine users whose primary fingers are incorrectly rejected, and
- $\text{FNMR}_T(t_1, t_2)$ is the fraction of genuine users for whom both fingers are rejected.

Note that in the results that follow we assume the single finger attempt time is fixed for all matchers. This blatantly ignores the card timing measurements of 5 which are less than 1 second for all but MX2M. While our intent is to show only the large effects of accuracy variations on time, we recommend that deployers should include these and other times in any formal or predictive model.

Note that this model assumes that the prior probability of impostors is small enough that their contribution to the aggregate transaction time is negligible.

We conduct two analyses, one in which $t_1 = t_2$, and a second in which the thresholds differ and are optimized to offer greater efficiency while maintaining an FMR objective. The determination of thresholds proceeds empirically:

---

[20]For example, authentication by a supervisor or via an alternative biometric modality.

| MX2D = Sagem Morpho | MX2E = Sagem Morpho | MX2G = Oberthur / id3 | MX2H = Oberthur / id3 |
| MX2I = Oberthur / id3 | MX2J = Oberthur / id3 | MX2K = Oberthur / id3 | MX2M = Giesecke - Devrient |

We use a global [21] search to find the (t_1, t_2) pair that minimizes the "cost" function τ_T while satisfying the overall security constraint $\text{FMR}_T \leq 0.001$, say.

4.7 Fusion results

We arbitrarily set $\tau_1 = 4$ seconds (i.e. the time for acquisition plus MATCH-ON-CARD processing of the first finger), $\tau_2 = 6$s (i.e. the times for a prompt, switch, acquisition plus processing of the second finger), and $\tau_r = 90$s (remedial authentication). NIST advances this model and set of parameters **only as an example** - any given operation should tailor such analysis specifically - and besides the actual τ values are irrelevant upto a multiplier. The result is a verification time that in many cases is exactly four seconds, but for some extends to 10 or 100 seconds.

For an overall FMR target of 0.001, we execute the model of eq. 9 for cases where $t_1 = t_2 = \text{FMR}^{-1}(0.0005)$ and where $t_1 \neq t_2$ are solved for to minimize cost. Table 9 shows the results from which the following observations can be made.

▷ Row one, column five shows that, for the most accurate matcher, the fraction of users needing to present a second finger is 3.06% when the thresholds are set to be equal.

▷ Row two, column five shows that, for the most accurate matcher, this fraction drops to 2.86% when the thresholds are allowed to float. The efficiency saving is larger for other implementations.

▷ This is achieved by lowering t_1 and elevating t_2. An added benefit is that the achieved overall FMR in column 6 is closer to the target FMR than for equal thresholds.

Table 10 summarizes the situation in which $t_1 = t_2 = t$ are set to achieve a target FMR of 0.0005 and users authenticate with their primary finger and only present their secondary finger if the first was rejected. Referring to Table 10(b), the results are:

▷ The FMR values are almost exactly doubled by allowing a second attempt;

▷ The FNMR values are reduced by factors between five and eleven;

▷ Together these differences are in agreement with the single-finger vs. sum-fused DET plots of Figure 1;

▷ The cells shaded green indicate that PIV compliance is possible with decision level fusion (at least for this particular matcher and template generator combination);

▷ The operational relevance of decision-level fusion is an improvement in efficiency: Not all users will have to present a secondary finger. In the case of MX2D cards and the particular template generator combination, only 3.86% of genuine users will have to submit their secondary finger.

▷ Score level fusion is slightly more accurate than decision level fusion.

None of the comparisons involved impostors presenting left as right, or vice versa.

4.8 Effect of discrete similarity scores

The effect of tied scores, as demonstrated in the latter rows of Table 10(a), is the failure to achieve the target FMR value of 0.0005. One remedy is to break ties by adding small amounts of noise to all scores:

$$s' = s + U(0, d/50) \tag{10}$$

---

[21] A global search for MX2D and MX2E was not possible because the large number of unique scores makes the naïve computation too costly. Instead we conducted a local search over a threshold range of $t_0 \pm 4000$ in increments of 5 about the point $t_0 = \text{FMR}^{-1}(0.0005)$. This entails 400^2 function evaluations.

| MX2D = Sagem Morpho | MX2E = Sagem Morpho | MX2G = Oberthur / id3 | MX2H = Oberthur / id3 |
| MX2I = Oberthur / id3 | MX2J = Oberthur / id3 | MX2K = Oberthur / id3 | MX2M = Giesecke - Devrient |

(a) Quality-assisted minutiae removal

Matcher	Generator		Comparisons		Pruning	FMR	FNMR
	Ref	Verify	Which	Number of	Priority		
MX2I	MX2D	B	All comparisons	2747804	Quality then radial	0.0018	0.0804
			Either or both templates have ≥ 61 minutiae	832225	Quality then radial	0.0013	0.1210
			Either or both templates have ≥ 61 minutiae	832225	Radial only	0.0013	0.1210
	MX2D	B	All comparisons	2747804	Quality then radial	0.0018	0.0804
			Either or both templates have ≥ 70 minutiae	194782	Quality then radial	0.0010	0.1817
			Either or both templates have ≥ 70 minutiae	194782	Radial only	0.0010	0.1816
	MX2D	MX2D	All comparisons	2747804	Quality then radial	0.0014	0.0574
			Either or both templates have ≥ 61 minutiae	491061	Quality then radial	0.0009	0.0612
			Either or both templates have ≥ 61 minutiae	491061	Radial only	0.0011	0.0693
	MX2D	MX2D	All comparisons	2747804	Quality then radial	0.0014	0.0574
			Either or both templates have ≥ 70 minutiae	79744	Quality then radial	0.0008	0.0769
			Either or both templates have ≥ 70 minutiae	79744	Radial only	0.0012	0.0992

(b) Center-assisted minutiae removal

Matcher	Generator		Comparisons		Pruned	FMR	FNMR
	Ref	Verify	Which	Number of	About		
MX2I	MX2Dq0	B	All comparisons	2747804	Dedicated (x_c, y_c)	0.0018	0.0803
			Either or both templates have ≥ 61 minutiae	832225	Dedicated (x_c, y_c)	0.0013	0.1210
			Either or both templates have ≥ 61 minutiae	832225	Center of Mass	0.0013	0.1209
	MX2Dq0	B	All comparisons	2747804	Dedicated (x_c, y_c)	0.0018	0.0803
			Either or both templates have ≥ 70 minutiae	194782	Dedicated (x_c, y_c)	0.0010	0.1816
			Either or both templates have ≥ 70 minutiae	194782	Center of Mass	0.0010	0.1815
	MX2Dq0	MX2Dq0	All comparisons	2747804	Dedicated (x_c, y_c)	0.0015	0.0588
			Either or both templates have ≥ 61 minutiae	491061	Dedicated (x_c, y_c)	0.0011	0.0693
			Either or both templates have ≥ 61 minutiae	491061	Center of Mass	0.0012	0.0608
	MX2Dq0	MX2Dq0	All comparisons	2747804	Dedicated (x_c, y_c)	0.0015	0.0588
			Either or both templates have ≥ 70 minutiae	79744	Dedicated (x_c, y_c)	0.0012	0.0992
			Either or both templates have ≥ 70 minutiae	79744	Center of Mass	0.0015	0.0752

Table 11: Effect of enhanced methods for minutiae removal.
The tables show the effect on FMR and FNMR of using minutia quality values and dedicated centers for removal of minutiae to satisfy MOC algorithm capability constraints. Throughout, the threshold is fixed at the (matcher-specific) value of 7 to give FMR near 0.001. The B generator does not emit quality values (per MINEX 04 requirements), and so its outputs are always pruned radially. In Table 10(a) the dedicated pruning center is used. In Table 10(b) the minutia quality values are zero throughout.

where U is a uniformly distributed noise process of zero mean and width $d/50$. The value of d is

$$d = \min_{i,j} |s_i - s_j| \qquad (11)$$

i.e. the smallest difference between any two matcher scores.

The effect of using equation 10 is to allow precise realization of the (higher) target FMR value, and to thereby reduce FNMR. This is evident by comparing values in columns four and five of Table 10(a) with the corresponding elements in Table 10(b).

4.9 Effect of using minutia quality values

The original MINEX 04 test required the minutia quality byte of the INCITS 378 record to be set to zero. This was done because it was considered that vendor values would be non-interoperable. In MINEX II, this requirement was dropped to allow quality values to be used to direct removal of minutiae. This process is part of the INCITS 378 to ISO/IEC 19794-2 COMPACT CARD conversion and is needed to strip excess minutiae from larger templates to satisfy the limits communicated by the card in its ISO/IEC 7816 BIT. The BIT parameters are listed in Table 12.

The evaluation plan [8] augmented the INCITS 378 definition of minutia quality to state that quality should be related to likelihood of the minutia being a true minutia (as opposed to a local ridge clarity measure, for example).

Vendor ID	Num BITs	Min	Max	Sort Order
MX2D	2	3	128	None Given (0x00)
MX2E	2	3	128	None Given (0x00)
MX2F	1	12	60	Y-X Ascending (0x09)
MX2G	1	12	60	Y-X Ascending (0x09)
MX2H	1	12	60	Y-X Ascending (0x09)
MX2I	1	12	60	Y-X Ascending (0x09)
MX2J	1	12	60	Y-X Ascending (0x09)
MX2K	1	12	60	Y-X Ascending (0x09)
MX2M	1	3	60	None Given (0x00)

Table 12: BIT parameters from the MINEX II cards.
In all cases, when a vendor's card had both BITs, they were identical.

Without quality values, the simplest mechanism for satisfying card cabability limits is to remove those with the largest radial distance from the center, as alluded to in ISO/IEC 19794-2:2005 .

$$r^2 = (x - x_c)^2 + (y - y_c)^2 \qquad (12)$$

This procedure was described in the evaluation plan [8]. To test the effectiveness of quality-directed pruning we applied only one of the 60-minutiae MATCH-ON-CARD implementations, MX2I. We generated a set of templates using the quality enabled MX2D minutia detector. We matched those against both MX2D templates and no-quality-value B templates. We then stripped the quality values from the MX2D templates, and rematched.

From the results shown in Table 10(a) the following observations can be made:

▷ The FNMR values are higher, and the FMR values are lower, when either or both of the input templates contain more than 60 minutiae i.e. $\max(N_r, N_v) > 60$. These effects are larger for very large templates i.e. $\max(N_r, N_v) > 70$.

▷ The quality-then-radial approach is superior to the radial-only method (i.e. eq. 12) only when both templates have minutia quality values (i.e. the MX2D-MX2D rows in the bottom half of the Table 10(a)). Refering to the last two lines, the effect is to reduce FNMR ($0.0992 \rightarrow 0.0769$).

▷ When one template is generated with quality values (MX2D) but the other does not (B) there is no gain in accuracy. Refering to the second block of three rows the effect on FNMR ($0.1817 \rightarrow 0.1816$) is negligible:

4.10 Effect of using dedicated centers for pruning

The MINEX II API[8] allowed the template generator to return the coordinates of a point about which minutiae should be removed. This was suggested by industry as an improvement over the use of the center-of-mass.

To assess whether this dedicated center was worthwhile, we again applied matcher MX2I to MX2D and B templates. The quality values were set to zero in all MX2D templates. Equation 12 was applied using either the specific (x_c, y_c) or the center of mass $(1/N \sum x_i, 1/N \sum y_i)$.

The results are shown in Table 10(b). We make the following observations.

▷ As with quality assisted pruning, there is essentially no change in accuracy when MX2D templates are compared with B templates.

▷ For MX2D-MX2D comparisons, there is a decrease in accuracy when templates are pruned about the dedicated center. Note that the minutia quality values were set to zero because otherwise minutia would be removed on the basis of low quality first and *then* on distance.

The conclusions on minutia removal this and the preceding section weakened by the following.

▷ Only one quality-equipped generator was available (MX2D) and it was used with only one other generator (B) and one matcher (MX2I).

▷ The negative result for the MX2D-B combination may be different for other template generators if they tend to produce more or fewer minutiae. This requires further testing.

▷ The comparison of templates from the same vendor may be rare in a large federated multivendor interoperable MATCH-ON-CARD application.

The results should not be considered as general until a wider survey of quality-enabled and center-enabled template generators can be conducted.

4.11 Card errors

All cards operated perfectly except that the MX2M card objected to the reference template PUT DATA command on 11 out of 80000 occasions. The error code in each case was 0x6F00.

4.12 Card-SDK differences

With two exceptions, all SDK and corresponding card-based matching implementations produced identical similarity scores given the same input template pairs. This was measured over 80000 comparisons. Identity of scores is the critical assurance that the on-card and off-card algorithms are identical.

The two exceptions were:

▷ MX2G which gave non-identical scores on 49 of 80000 comparisons. These all occured on low-scoring impostor comparisons, and the absolute score difference never exceeded 3. This means that about 0.06% of impostor and approximately 0.02% of genuine comparisons gave different SDK and Card values.

▷ Whenever the MX2M sdk produced a similarity score of 7 or below, the MX2M card reported 0. This means that about 84% of impostor and approximately 5% of genuine comparisons gave different SDK and Card values. The consequence of this disparity is that NIST cannot conclude that the same algorithm is in use, and would not test it for compliance to the PIV accuracy specification.

5 MOC timing

5.1 Measurement techniques

For each card submitted, NIST measured the duration of all executions of the following actions.

▷ Reference template storage operations made using the PUT_DATA APDU,

▷ Template comparisons using the VERIFY APDU which includes the sending of the verification template to the card, and

▷ The similarity score retrieval operations made via the GET_DATA APDU.

The time taken to generate the verification template is not included in the above. For the MX2D generator, the median time to convert an in-memory uncompressed greyscale raster image into an INCITS 378 record was 0.11 seconds. The 99-th percentile time was 0.19 seconds. These times apply to Xeon-based PCs.

| MX2D = Sagem Morpho | MX2E = Sagem Morpho | MX2G = Oberthur / id3 | MX2H = Oberthur / id3 |
| MX2I = Oberthur / id3 | MX2J = Oberthur / id3 | MX2K = Oberthur / id3 | MX2M = Giesecke - Devrient |

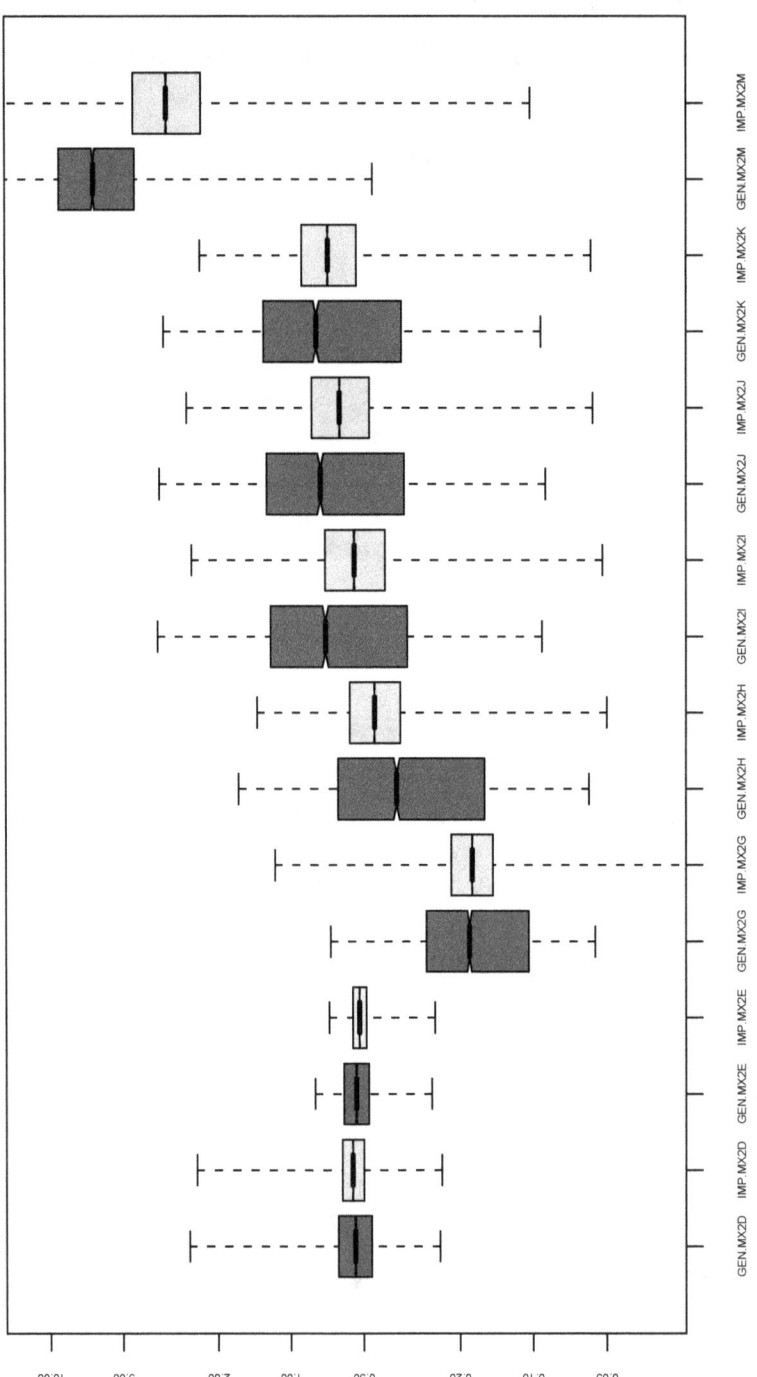

Figure 2: Times for ISO/IEC 7816 VERIFY commands to complete for all MINEX II cards and broken out for genuine and impostor comparisons. Genuine comparisons are shown in green, impostors in yellow.

| MX2D = Sagem Morpho | MX2E = Sagem Morpho | MX2G = Oberthur / id3 | MX2H = Oberthur / id3 |
| MX2I = Oberthur / id3 | MX2J = Oberthur / id3 | MX2K = Oberthur / id3 | MX2M = Giesecke - Devrient |

These times were measured by means of the Linux *gettimeofday()* system call. The NIST card test driver wraps each APDU in two such calls, and the interval is obtained by subtraction. This is shown in the driver source code, which may be downloaded and inspected via the NIST open-source server (see BIOMAPP, section 3.7).

While the *gettimeofday()* call offers better than microsecond resolution on the platform we used for testing, the measured durations include more than just the elemental card operations. The overhead includes these

▷ all the calls to the PC/SC library,

▷ communication from the card driver process to the PC/SC smartcard daemon, and

▷ USB communication.

The effect of these is assumed to be fixed across all MATCH-ON-CARD implementations tested. In particular, the host computer was dedicated to the testing of the cards, with only normal operating system related and file system processes running. These processes require very little overhead in terms of overall system resources.

The hardware listed in Appendix A was disclosed to participants before the test. MINEX II did not test other configurations, and while we understand that faster end-to-end times may be possible using alternative hardware and protocols, the timing method used here is fair and consistent for comparison of implementations.

5.2 Comparison timing results

Figure 2 is a boxplot summary of the time taken by the various MATCH-ON-CARD implementations to execute the ISO/IEC 7816 VERIFY command. The plot separates the genuine from impostor comparisons. The colored boxes indicate the interquartile range. The whiskers indicate the extreme values. The plots are derived from 80000 comparisons for each matcher. Of those 5012 correspond to genuine comparisons. Regarding the VERIFY command, we make the following observations.

▷ The most accurate MATCH-ON-CARD algorithm, MX2D, is neither the slowest, nor the fastest. The median time for the execution of genuine VERIFY command is 0.54 seconds. Only about 1% of the 80000 comparisons exceeds 0.77 seconds.

▷ MX2E, the less accurate sibling of MX2D, is not appreciably faster. However, the variance and worst-case times are reduced.

▷ For the fastest implementation, MX2G, the median time for the execution of genuine VERIFY command is 0.18 seconds.

▷ Across all matchers, the median VERIFY time never exceeds 0.8 seconds.

▷ The VERIFY time distributions are approximately Normal (Q-Q plots are linear to beyond $+3\sigma$). However, outliers do occur and these are *not* measurement errors attributable to the testing platform. Instead there are a small number of templates that are problematic for multiple suppliers' matchers. For example, one template involved in the second-slowest MX2D comparison (2.45 seconds) also causes comparisons in excess of two seconds for matchers MX2I, MX2J and MX2K.

▷ In all cases, the variance of the genuine comparisons is larger than that of impostor comparisons.

5.3 Other timing results

We also measured the times required to place a reference template on the card and to retrieve the similarity score from the card. These are summarized as boxplots in Figures 3(a) and 3(b). Both of these are unimportant: population of the card happens once at time of card issuance, and retrieval is a test-specific function, and never part of an operational authentication attempt. The retrieval time is interesting here because it reveals the variation inherent in the card-PC communication for the retrieval of a fixed size data object (8 bytes). Over all matchers, $2\sigma = 0.007$ seconds.

| MX2D = Sagem Morpho | MX2E = Sagem Morpho | MX2G = Oberthur / id3 | MX2H = Oberthur / id3 |
| MX2I = Oberthur / id3 | MX2J = Oberthur / id3 | MX2K = Oberthur / id3 | MX2M = Giesecke - Devrient |

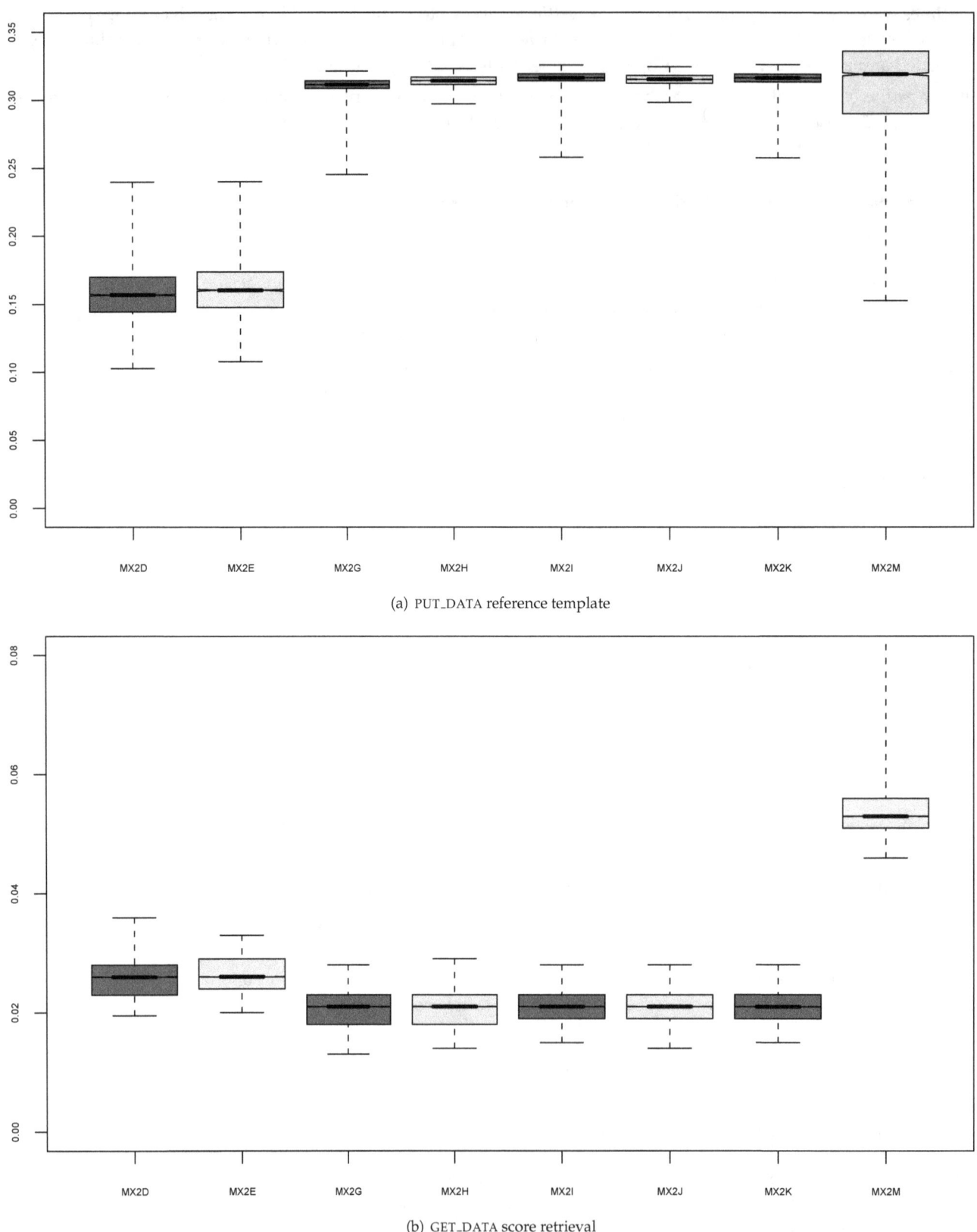

Figure 3: Times in seconds for ISO/IEC 7816 APDUs for storage of the reference template on the card, and for retrieval of the similarity scores from the card.

| MX2D = Sagem Morpho | MX2E = Sagem Morpho | MX2G = Oberthur / id3 | MX2H = Oberthur / id3 |
| MX2I = Oberthur / id3 | MX2J = Oberthur / id3 | MX2K = Oberthur / id3 | MX2M = Giesecke - Devrient |

6 Non-conformance to the MINEX II specification

The MINEX II test specification worked very well. That is, SDK implementations conformed to both the API, and the cards conformed to the required APDUs. That said, we document below the few irregularities we had to work around.

1. The Biometric Header Template (BHT), contained within the Biometric Information Template (BIT), has several mandatory fields as required by ISO/IEC 7816-11:2004 . Two fields, format owner (TLV tag 0x87) and format type (tag 0x87) are specified in the MINEX II test document has having values 0x0101 and 0x005, respectively. One vendor omitted those fields, with this justification:

   > *The CBEFF info, tags 0x87 and 0x88 within the BHT are actually missing because we believed it was the default value as described in Note 6 of Table C1 of 7816-11.*

   However, Note 6 in Table C1 of the MINEX II Evaluation Plan[8] refers to the OID of the CBEFF standard body field (tag 0x06) only, not the format owner and format type fields, which are noted as mandatory. This fact was pointed out to the vendor, and we received this response:

   > *You are correct and the note 6 of table C1 applies only to the 0x06 tag in the BIT, not the 0x87 and 0x88 tags in the BHT. Our reading assumed that the logic behind note 6 could also applied to the 0x87 and 0x88 tags in the BHT and that the editor forgot to extend the note 6 to these 2 tags of similar nature. But we can easily add these 2 tags in the next card delivery.*

   This was done. In order to proceed with testing, we modified the NIST test driver to ignore the absence of these fields. Future testing within the MINEX II framework will require the presence of these fields.

2. Card and Matcher IDs in the TLV objects: The MINEX II test specification defined the APDUs and expected responses for reading card and matcher IDs. The GET DATA instruction code (0xCB) is used, and the Lc field contains a tag list data object (code 0x5C), requesting a single TLV data item to be returned. The requested object ID for the card ID is 0x66, and for the matcher ID is 0x6E.

   The MINEX II Evaluation Plan[8] states that the returned data object should be of the form "0x73 06 88 04 <4 byte CBEFF ID>", which is non-conforming with regard to ISO 7816 use of the 0x5C code, in that the returned data object's tag should be the same as that requested. Therefore, the correct response for the card ID is "0x66 08 73 06 88 04 <4 byte card ID>", and for the matcher ID is "0x6E 08 73 06 99 04 <4 byte matcher ID>".

   One vendor returned the data object in the correct (i.e. NOT according to the MINEX II document) form; all other cards returned the IDs in the form given in the document. NIST changed the test software to accept either form so testing could proceed. Future versions of the MINEX II will be corrected, and cards should return data objects in the ISO-compliant format.

   An improvement to the test specification is to use a single APDU to request both the card and matcher IDs to be returned in the application related data object: The APDU would be the same as currently used for matcher ID: "0x00 CB 3F FF 03 5C 01 6E 00"

   The response data object would be: "0x6E 0E 73 0C 88 04 <4 byte card ID> 99 04 <4 byte matcher ID>"

   Another alternative is to ask for both card and matcher IDs to be returned in a single response. The APDU would be: "0x00 CB 3f FF 04 5C 02 66 6E"

   with this response: "0x66 08 73 06 88 04 <4 byte card ID> 6E 08 73 06 99 04 <4 byte matcher ID>"

7 References

References

[1] Working Group 1. Standing Document 2 Harmonized Biometric Vocabulary. Technical report, ISO/IEC JTC1 SC37 N1248, November 2005.

[2] Working Group 5. *ISO/IEC 19795-1 Biometric Performance Testing and Reporting: Principles and Framework*. JTC1 :: SC37, international standard edition, August 2005. http://isotc.iso.org/isotcportal.

[3] W.-Y. Choi, K. Lee, S.B. Pan, and Y. Chung. Realizable classifiers: Improving performance on variable cost problems. In M. H. Hamza, editor, *BMVC*. ACTA Press, 2004.

[4] D. Cooper, H. Dang, P. Lee, W. MacGregor, and K. Mehta. Secure Biometric Match-on-Card Feasibility Report. Technical report, National Institute of Standards and Technology, November 2007. Published as NIST Interagency Report 7452.

[5] J. Campbell et al. *ILO Seafarers' Identity Documents Biometric Testing Campaign Report*. International Labour Organization, Geneva, 2005. http://www.ilo.org/public/english/dialogue/sector/papers/maritime/sid-test-report2.pdf.

[6] T. Mansfield et al. Research report on minutiae interoperability tests. Technical report, Minutiae Template Interoperability Testing, 2007. http://www.mtitproject.com/DeliverableD62.pdf.

[7] P. Grother, M. McCabe, C. Watson, M. Indovina, W. Salamon, P. Flanagan, E. Tabassi, E. Newton, and C. Wilson. Performance and Interoperability of the INCITS 378 Fingerprint Template. Technical report, National Institute of Standards and Technology, March 2006. Published as NIST Interagency Report 7296.

[8] P. Grother and W. Salamon. Minex ii - an assessment of iso/iec 7816 card-based match-on-card capabilities - evaluation plan. Technical Report NISTIR 7477, National Institute of Standards and Technology, fingerprint.nist.gov/minexII/, August 2007.

[9] A. K. Jain, S. Prabhakar, and S. Chen. Combining combining multiple matchers for a high security fingerprint verification system. *Pattern Recognition Letters*, 20(3):1371–1379, March 1999.

[10] J. Kittler, M. Hatef, R. Duin, and J. Matas. On combining classifiers. *IEEE Trans. Pattern Analysis and Machine Intelligence*, 20(3), March 1998.

[11] I. B. Perelle and L. Ehrman. An international study of human handedness: The data. *Behavior Genetetics*, 24(3):217–227, May 1994.

[12] M. J. J. Scott, N. Niranjan, and R. W. Prager. Svm-based speaker verification algorithm for match-on-card. In John N. Carter and Mark S. Nixon, editors, *BMVC*. British Machine Vision Association, 1998.

[13] R. Snelick, U. Uludag, A. Mink, M. Indovina, and A. Jain. Large scale evaluation of multimodal biometric authentication using state-of-the-art systems. *IEEE Trans. Pattern Analysis and Machine Intelligence*, 27(3):450–455, March 2005.

[14] E. Tabassi, G. W. Quinn, and P. Grother. When to fuse two biometrics. In *Proceedings of IEEE Conference on Computer Vision and Pattern Recognition*. Workshop on Biometrics, June 2006. See http://fingerprint.nist.gov/minexII/CVPR06contingentfusion.pdf.

A Hardware used

The testing software used on the NIST test systems is comprised of several layers: The NIST test driver; the PC/SC library; the PC/SC daemon; and the USB device drivers. The NIST test driver is part of the BIOMAPP project, described above. The operating system used was RedHat Enterprise Linux 4.

The PC/SC software used is part of the M.U.S.C.L.E. (www.linuxnet.com) project developing smartcard solutions for the Linux, OS-X, and Solaris operating systems. Many Linux distributions include the pcsclite package, comprising the PC/SC library and daemon. The smartcard reader driver used was the generic CCID driver. We initially used version 1.3.7 of the pcsc-lite driver (the default under Redhat 5) but migrated to version 1.4.0 after it was found that the older version added a nearly constant delay to all APDU calls. The newer version was used for all times reported herein.

Testing was done on dual-CPU Intel Xeon based blade computers, running at 2.80 GHz. Each system has 2G of RAM. The smartcard reader is the SCR 335 produced by SCM Microsystems, with a USB interface, and is CCID compliant. This reader supports T=0 and T=1 protocols, 7816 Class A and AB cards, up to 8 MHz.

B Audit information

Study	MINEX II PHASE II
Report generated	Fri Feb 29 10:08:21 2008
Report name	minex_report.tex
Report last modified	Fri Feb 29 10:08:19 2008
Report MD5 hexadecimal	b9e5335a8d58c5e744327978e63df368
NIST contact	minexII@nist.gov

| MX2D = Sagem Morpho | MX2E = Sagem Morpho | MX2G = Oberthur / id3 | MX2H = Oberthur / id3 |
| MX2I = Oberthur / id3 | MX2J = Oberthur / id3 | MX2K = Oberthur / id3 | MX2M = Giesecke - Devrient |

www.ingramcontent.com/pod-product-compliance
Lightning Source LLC
Chambersburg PA
CBHW081815170526
45167CB00008B/3446